W. T. Currie BA

Brodie's Notes on Samuel Beckett's

Waiting for Godot

Pan Educational London and Sydney

First published 1978 by Pan Books Ltd
Cavaye Place, London SW10 9PG
1 2 3 4 5 6 7 8 9
© W. T. Currie 1978
ISBN 0 330 50072 4
Filmset in Great Britain by
Northumberland Press Ltd, Gateshead, Tyne and Wear
Printed and bound by
Richard Clay (The Chaucer Press) Ltd, Bungay, Suffolk

Contents

Page references in these Notes are to the Faber paperback edition of *Waiting for Godot*, but as each Act is analysed separately in the textual notes and elsewhere, these Notes may be used with any edition of the play

Introduction

The history of the British theatre in the 1950s is exciting. Things were happening on the stage and in the minds of the playwrights that hadn't happened since the early stirrings of drama, when this form of expression was new.

For one thing, there were suddenly, it seemed, hundreds of new dramatists. Whereas formerly the art had been left to a few established and reliable writers, now the field was wide open. To cater for the new outpouring, small theatre clubs, more or less esoteric in nature, grew up and flourished or faded quickly, as support for them waxed or waned. Every kind of script was sent to these clubs, and every kind of label given to their work. These names varied from 'kitchen-sink' drama to 'the theatre of the absurd'. There certainly wasn't one label that fitted the whole gamut of the plays. Theatre critics were bewildered by the situation, totally unsure of their ground and unwilling to risk too trenchant critical comment for fear that their own ignorance should be exposed. It is always interesting to look back at critical comments made, by contemporaries, on any new genre. Every age has produced its gloriously wild statement about a play that has turned out to be a masterpiece a few generations ahead.

The main cause of bewilderment was that the old critical tenets of Aristotle and the ideas of a well-made play with carefully developed plot and character-delineation no longer seemed to apply. The fall of a great man through some fatal flaw of character was no longer relevant. For one thing, there were no great men to be found in these plays. Here were tramps, misfits, outcasts from society, and they had already fallen as far as they could. Character seemed too fine a word to use of them, and they hardly appeared sufficiently universal to be symbols. The theatre no longer seemed a comfortable place to be. There were too many shocks, both to sensibility and to prejudice. If Bernard Shaw had stunned a generation of theatre-goers with his 'Not bloody likely!' of *Pygmalion*, here was shock a hundredfold. Pimps, panders and prostitutes were the new stage-walkers, and their language fitted their personalities.

There was a shift too of background. The complacent, suburban home with its middle-class standards was no longer sufficient to hold the attention of an audience. It demanded and got stronger meat. Every aspect of life was looked at as closely as beneath a microscope, and unpleasant things were discovered under stones. Indeed, it is here that the dramatists are most held up to censure. It is all very well moving stones, but there must be some answer to the problems that we reveal in the move. These young dramatists – for most of them were in their early twenties – asked plenty of questions, made many revelations, but did not appear to give any answers or suggest any remedies. It is not really sufficient for them to imply that their task is simply to point things out, and to leave the remedy to others.

There were still plays being written and produced with conventional construction and comfortable plot, but perhaps a few critical comments from the time may help underline the general attitude to the new offerings:

'of a badness that must be called indescribable.' *The Times*.
'a masterpiece of meaningless significance.' *Punch*.
'another frightful ordeal.' *The Sunday Times*.

These comments were made about Whiting's *Saint's Day*, Pinter's *The Birthday Party* and Arden's *Serjeant Musgrave's Dance* respectively. It has taken us nearly a quarter of a century to come to terms with this 'new' drama.

Looking back to that time, it is no wonder that students of modern drama find a new starting-point in the small Théâtre Babylone on the Paris Left Bank. With *Waiting for Godot*, (first published in the French language, (as *En attendant Godot*) in 1952 by Les Éditions de Minuit) Beckett was to give them something that was quite new, something startling yet acceptable to the extent that within a decade the play had become a classic in its own kind. This new convention of drama had been copied, parodied, translated and produced in a variety of forms and in a great number of languages. In its turn it had become established, although arguments about interpretation still raged. The truly remarkable thing was that opinion was not left to a few select people in avant-garde groups; the wider theatrical, and indeed the cinema-going, public had an opportunity to judge for itself.

Regarded dispassionately, the play seems far too obscure to have had so much time spent in attacking it, or in extolling its merits. Unless we study it closely, it appears to have been concocted rather than planned. Character and plots, as we have said, fly in the face of all that Aristotle demanded of them. The basic ingredient of any work of art appears to be lacking, so that communication itself is almost wilfully clouded. This holds, not only between the author and ourselves, but between the characters as well in their relationships with each other. There is an almost perverse desire to hide meaning in a welter of half-statements and stifled thoughts. A sound critical maxim, however, is to be prepared to make the same intellectual effort to understand a work of imagination as the author did to compose it. By following this advice here we may begin to be aware of the complex structure that faces us in the play. Perhaps we don't, in fact, have to go to such depths for full understanding, or it may be that, as with most works of real worth, there are different levels of awareness. Martin Esslin tells us that when a touring company acted before the prisoners of San Quentin gaol, San Francisco, they had no doubt about the real point of the play. They saw it as being about 'the release that never came'. They understood only too well the tedium of waiting and the promise that was never fulfilled. So, basically we have a germinal play, revolutionary in concept and startling in character. Tom Milne relates plays like it to the *théâtre maudit* of France, where only a few 'adventurous minds', as he calls them, will be prepared to make the effort to understand. Perhaps this may have been the case with the first audiences, but it is certainly not so now.

A more traditional modern dramatist, Christopher Fry, put the problem that must have faced Beckett quite clearly when he said, 'Two hundred years ago the dramatist knew how to approach the stage. Now the writer may find the lack of a universal manner a disadvantage.'

Subsequent dramatists have been taking whatever they found helpful from this play of Beckett's, rarely bothering even to acknowledge the debt. In our critical reading we will find as wide a variety of comment as we find plays within this modern period. The same mixture of styles that Shakespeare mocked is still with us, but Beckett has at least taught us not to look for narrative in our theatre. From this play on, the idea of drama as action and story no longer applied. The writer had a new dimension to work in. Silence too was rediscovered as a positive quality, and we do not have to look far in *Godot* to see how Beckett exploits this in the attitudes of Vladimir and Estragon. In their moments of total silence these two scarecrows on the verge of humanity do rouse in us feelings of compassion, and Robert Shaw underlines this when he says, 'Compassion's the thing. That's why I think I like *Waiting for Godot* more than anything I've seen since the war. I don't know why so many people call it a depressing play. Beckett writes about suffering in a way that makes me feel exhilarated – that I must get up and go out and do what I can.'

For one author at least, then, the message of the play is 'something must be done'. Finally, however, this message is the play itself.

Some further useful critical quotations

I'd be quite incapable of writing a critical introduction to my own works. Beckett

I began to write Godot as a relaxation from the awful prose I was writing at that time. Beckett

I have been brooding in my bath for the last hour and have come to the conclusion that the success of *Waiting for Godot* means the end of the theatre as we know it. Robert Morley

Beckett told me that Godot was a grand-piano. Peter Bull in a BBC broadcast.

Waiting for Godot is 'about' two destitutes hopefully awaiting the promised arrival of a third, and not daring to move in case they miss him. Popular view of the play The idea that Beckett is a uniformly depressing writer is a misconception. Martin Esslin

He is uplifting, exhilarating in the theatre. For an actor, to explore his compassion and his lyricism is very satisfying. Jack MacGowran

He [Beckett] strips his figures so thoroughly of all those qualities in which the audience might recognize itself that to start with, an alienation effect is created that leaves the audience mystified. Dr Metman

Now the audience ... wants to be entertained rather than disturbed, wants to be comforted and really doesn't want any kind of adventure in the theatre, at least from living playwrights. Edward Albee

Godot is a great play. Bernard Levin

Play architecture as it was understood by the writer of the well-made play . . . has given place to a seemingly abstract void in which plot, or dramatic story-telling, is almost non-existent. Hugh Hunt

The theatre of the absurb is 'a theatre of situation as against a theatre of events in sequence'. Martin Esslin

The author and his work

'The author is never interesting.' (Beckett)

Samuel Beckett was born in Dublin on 13 April 1906. His childhood was reasonably happy, though he confesses he had 'little talent for happiness'. At school he was academically brilliant (later he was to take the best First of his year at University), and competent at most games, particularly rugby and cricket. He read for a degree in Modern Languages, and became a lecturer in English at the École Normale Supérieure in Paris, and later in French at Trinity College, Dublin.

From 1932 he lived chiefly in France, and was for a while secretary to James Joyce. They shared a delight in language, and were both absorbed by the problems of communication.

His early poetry and first three novels (of which the very first, *Dream of Fair to Middling Women*, remains unpublished) were written in English, but the trilogy *Molloy*, *Malone meurt* and *L'Innommable* was written in French, as were *En Attendant Godot* and *Fin de Partie* (End Game). *Godot* gives us an insight into Beckett's view of human nature, with its lack of hope and the inability of the characters to make any positive move to help themselves.

As a writer Beckett is unmoved by public acclaim or the popular idea of 'success', but he accepted graciously and without demur the award of the Nobel Prize for Literature in 1969.

Further reading

Studies of Beckett and his work

Duckworth, Colin *Angels of Darkness: Dramatic Effects in Beckett and Ionesco* (Allen & Unwin)

Duckworth, Colin (editor) *En attendant Godot*, original French text of play, with 100-page introduction in English (Harrap)

Esslin, Martin (editor) *Samuel Beckett: A collection of Critical Essays* (Prentice-Hall, New Jersey)

Fletcher, John *Waiting for Godot*, edition with notes, (Faber and Faber)

Hayman, Ronald *Samuel Beckett* (Heinemann)

Jacobsen, J. and Mueller, W. R. *The Testament of Samuel Beckett* (Faber)

Kenner, Hugh *Samuel Beckett* (Calder)

Reid, Alec *All I Can Manage, More Than I Could: An Approach to the Plays of Samuel Beckett* (The Dolmen Press)

Robinson, Michael *The Long Sonata of the Dead. A study of Samuel Beckett* (Rupert Hart-Davis)

Scott, Nathan A. *Samuel Beckett* (Bowes and Bowes)

Tindall, W. *Samuel Beckett* (Columbia University Press, New York)

Contemporary Theatre

Brown, J. R. and Harris B. (editors) *Contemporary Theatre, Stratford-on-Avon Studies No. 4* (Edward Arnold)

Esslin, Martin *The Theatre of the Absurd* (Eyre and Spottiswoode)

Hunt, Hugh *The Live Theatre* (Oxford University Press)

Pronko, L. C. *Avant-Garde: The Experimental Theatre in France* (University of California Press, California)

Styan, J. L. *The Dark Comedy: The Development of Modern Comic Tragedy* (Cambridge University Press)

Philosophy and meaning of the play

Philosophy

There is a danger of our becoming lost if we spend too much time in trying to probe the philosophy behind the work. Beckett does not acknowledge the influence of any one particular philosophy more than another in the play. There is, however, a good deal of the mystic about the author, and this is reflected in his characters. He does, after all, take one of the central moments of the Christian belief, the Crucifixion, as a starting-point in one of his philosophical digressions, and, although the mystical approach may not always be specifically Christian, it can frequently be termed religious.

Since Beckett was writing in Paris, and in view of his play's date, it is not surprising that his ideas should be linked with those of Sartre and the philosophy with which he was associated, Existentialism. This was a way of thinking that moved counter to the traditional view of Plato. The Platonists believed that whatever was good and beautiful reflected a particle of the supreme goodness and beauty. In *Adonais*, Shelley, writing of the dead Keats, suggests that he is now part of the loveliness which 'Once he made more lovely.' In other words, he is now one with the supreme essence. The Existentialists denied the existence of this supreme state, and said that eternal truths were illusion, and that it was for the individual to work out his salvation. Experience was what counted, and its nature determined our characters. It was up to each one of us, therefore, to seek our own identity. If we look at the rest of Beckett's writing we find that this search for identity is a recurrent theme. In *Endgame* the father and mother in their dustbins look back to their lost youth, when they rode tandem on their honeymoon. Malone, in the novel

Malone Dies, desperately seeks his identity as he lies dying. Perhaps, however, the theme is most obvious in *Krapp's Last Tape* as the hero listens to the tape of his youthful voice, whose message he fails to comprehend and which he is unable to identify.

There is no reason, therefore, to dismiss this theme of Beckett's simply because the characters he chooses to delineate are at the lower end of human society. Their search for identity is as valid as our own, and their quest perhaps made more poignant by the depths they have plumbed.

Meaning

As with the interpretation of Godot himself, the author steadfastly refused to be drawn into discussion over the meaning of the work. In 1956, however, he did hint that the great success of the play had been due to the fact that the public had insisted on 'imposing allegorical and symbolic meaning on a play which was striving to avoid definition'. One is tempted to ask what else he expected them to do, as without those imposed meanings we have a pretty incomprehensible farrago. Even with them appreciation of the work is not easy.

The first audiences in America were bewildered by the play, chiefly as it had been billed as the comedy hit of Europe. (Students will note that it is classed as A Tragicomedy in two Acts). They were making for the exits in droves long before the interval. Those who stayed, however, might have realized that they were watching something very significant. As one critic suggested, 'Godot gave the theatre a new starting point.'

There have been as many interpretations of the play as there have been critics, and no doubt further theories will be added to the store as time goes on. Kay Boyle, for example, worked out an elaborate analogy between the play and Beckett's stay in France during the war. (His return to that troubled region was itself a kind of perversity.) She pointed to the end of the second Act, with its reference to the Pyrenees, and likened that to the escape route used by the prisoners during the German Occupation. Beckett himself said there wasn't a word of truth in it; though, as she adds 'He has never held that, or anything else, against me.'

At any rate, here is a play that we cannot ignore, interpret it as we may. The author, from his self-imposed isolation in Paris emerges to give instruction and advice to producers of the play, and no doubt every production adds a little more to our understanding of its meaning. Beckett has pointed the way with his work, and we must follow as we can.

One interpretation of the play is the equation of Vladimir, with the body, and Estragon with the mind, and the action of the one upon the other. Beckett himself recognized this duality (he calls it pseudocouple, the splitting of self). His reading of the philosophy of Arnold Geulincx (1624–69) encouraged him in this line of thought, and it is interesting for us to follow the links through to *Waiting for Godot*. Basically the philosopher posits that the body and soul are distinct parts of our being, and the God has control only of the body. We are able to control our own minds. The more perceptive among us consequently fall back on mental processes that we can manipulate for ourselves. The fact that the body can act under the mind's stimulus is explained by Geulincx in the terms of two clocks that synchronize whilst remaining independent. Colin Duckworth sees this as the reason for the tramps' inability to go to Pozzo's aid when he falls in the second Act. Their time-scale has got out of phase, and they are unable to carry out the simplest physical movement.

Plot and themes

Plot

There is virtually no plot in *Waiting for Godot*: it could perhaps best be described as the dilemma of two characters. Beckett has placed his two tramps (or clowns) in a situation from which there is no escape, unless through the mind. They are tied to the one place, reduced to the basics of human need and incapable of positive action as individuals, so dependent are they on each other. They are not even able to fetch a rope for their own suicide, for that would imply a separation which they cannot face. When they do part for short spells their reunion is touching, almost painful.

It is the escape through suicide that is given most prominence in the play. They have tried it before, and thought about it often. Towards the end of the first Act, as they think about fetching a piece of rope for hanging themselves, Estragon remarks, 'Do you remember the day I threw myself into the Rhône?' and Vladimir replies, 'That's all dead and buried . . . There's no good harking back on that.'

The attempt to escape through suicide at the end of the second Act is no more successful. The cord which holds up Estragon's trousers isn't strong enough.

They each take an end of the cord and pull. It breaks. They almost fall.

So, they continue to wait, and we are left to resolve their dilemma in our own way. The author demands that we share their situation with them; we cannot simply ignore it, for we are part of it. As John Donne wrote, 'No man is an island entire of itself.'

Themes

Beckett has said that he finds drama relaxing for him: 'You have a definite space and People in this space. That's relaxing.' Within the confines of the stage he is able to touch on a number of themes without necessarily coming to any conclusion about them. He leaves each of us to work out our own conclusion. The plan of the play is cyclical, and we keep returning to our starting-point. This idea is echoed in Vladimir's song at the beginning of Act 2, in the mournful dirge that could go on for ever about the death of a dog whose saga is perpetuated on its tombstone for all the other dogs to read ad infinitum. It is the same theme as we find in T. S. Eliot, (in the first line of 'East Coker') 'in my beginning is my end', and nowhere do we find it more powerfully expressed than in the 'birth over a grave' image later in the play.

Repentance and Salvation

Vladimir sees hope for them in repentance for sin: 'Suppose we repented'. Estragon, however, sees their only fault as that of having been born. 'Repented what? . . . Our being born?' The guffaw with which Vladimir greets this statement is swiftly stifled, and his face becomes a mask of emotions that are turned on and off at will. Estragon, the cynic, constantly stops Vladimir in his tracks as he demands explanations of self-evident terms like 'Saviour' and 'Hell'. Yet, as we have said, it is he who dismisses general opinion as not being worthy of attention.

Neither tramp is able to seek salvation from a position of strength. They are abject creatures putting forward 'A vague supplication', and on their hands and knees at that. They are also constantly afraid, and when they think Godot is coming they huddle together for comfort.

There is a kind of lottery about their hopes of salvation. All four writers of the Gospels had witnessed the Crucifixion, yet only one mentioned the salvation of one of the thieves.

Vladimir takes this as significant, while Estragon dismisses it as a vagary of the Gospel-writer. They do, however, accept the odds of being saved as quite high. After all, one of the thieves was saved, and there are two of them. Perhaps their fear and reluctance to break off their friendship depends on this. They may be loath to risk discovering which of them is to be saved.

Time

Time and its passing is a recurrent topic in the conversation of the tramps. The hours are tedious until Godot comes, but they must be passed somehow. Talk is called for, and an element of intellectual discussion. The pressing needs of nature are attended to, and this gives the illusion of action – something is being achieved. Food is a palliative and a further time-killer. It can be discussed, and the merits of one root vegetable set against another. Pozzo and Lucky create a diversion which sets the tramps off on further lines of thought to beguile them in their interminable wait. It is in fact Pozzo who in the first Act rejects Vladimir's charge 'Time has stopped', as he listens to the ticking of his watch and so refutes this blasphemy. Although Vladimir points out that the hours are long, there is some hope, as he remarks in Act 2, 'Time flows again already. The sun will set, the moon will rise, and we away . . . from here' (p.77).

Meanwhile there are further pastimes. The tramps can mime the episode of Pozzo and Lucky; they can re-enact it in fantasy. They can also revile one another in bitter invective, rising (or stooping) to the final insult: 'Crritic!' But this has gone too far even for Vladimir, as we hear the dismay of his 'Oh!', and read the stage-direction *He wilts, vanquished, and turns away*. All the characters in the play are vague about when yesterday was and when tomorrow will be. Was it really 'a million years ago, in the nineties' when the then presentable pair, Vladimir and Estragon, might have hurled themselves to destruction from the top of the Eiffel Tower? Will they really come back 'tomorrow', and will that morrow see Godot's arrival?

Place

The tramps are constantly trying to identify their rendezvous. There is repeated doubt about whether they are at the right spot or not. It is through an attempt at such identification that we find the only visible symbolic change in the play – the sprouting of the leaves on the tree. This latter is the only obvious prop on stage when we meet the two tramps, and it is quickly drawn to our notice. There is a crisis of identity about it, as to whether it is a tree, a bush, alive or dead, and even what kind of tree it is. The idea of place is vague so far as the two are concerned, and they will not commit themselves to any accurate identification. Vladimir puts it into words with his angry 'Nothing is certain when you are about.' Throughout the play directions are given in either a flippant or solicitous tone, while the static and inactive is emphasized:

Pozzo 'I don't seem able . . . (*long hesitation*) . . . to depart.'

In the second Act Vladimir taunts Estragon with his inability to remember and to recognize their location; this rouses him to the bitter rejoinder, 'What is there to recognize? All my lousy life I've crawled about in the mud! And you talk to me about scenery! . . . Look at this muckheap! I've never stirred from it!' (p.61). As the conversation continues, and the sprouting of leaves on the tree causes comment, Estragon refutes the fact that they have ever been there before, and Vladimir seizes eagerly on this one point of agreement. It is the presence of the boots, however, that causes further doubt, but are they really Estragon's boots? Determined to orientate themselves, Vladimir theorizes about the footwear and reaches the (for him) satisfactory conclusion that that was where Estragon had been sitting the previous evening. It is another item of clothing, however, that clinches the identification of place, namely Lucky's hat. There is no gainsaying that monstrosity, and hope once more dawns.

Night and the Dark

The coming of night with the attendant suggestion of oblivion is one of the play's most frequent allusions. Vladimir asks repeatedly if night will never come, Pozzo says that if he had their task he would wait till it was black night before he gave up, and there is the sinister overtone, 'But night does not fall.'

This is a twilight play; it could not face the full glare of noon. Act 1 has the laconic setting, *A country road. A tree. Evening.* Act 2 could not be more precise or repetitive – *Next Day. Same time. Same Place.* It is night with its suggestion of release, or at least rest, that the two tramps seek, and it is this as well as the arrival of Godot that they await. Vladimir links the two ideas in Act 2 with the entrance of Lucky and the blind Pozzo. Feeble as the two are, he sees them as reinforcements, and knows that somehow their presence will ensure the survival of Estragon and himself. The company of other humans means that they 'are no longer alone, waiting for the night . . . It's tomorrow.' But, of course, it is not. They are still chained to circumstance, unable to move far, and with dawn stifled in its birth.

Food

Estragon never quite gets what he asks for the first time. A carrot is mysteriously transformed into a turnip and angrily rejected, but in the end the desired food is discovered and the carrot produced. The longer he eats it, however, the worse the taste is, but Vladimir asserts the contrary:

Estragon Funny, the more you eat the worse it gets.
Vladimir With me it's the opposite.

When Pozzo and Lucky appear later in the same Act much is made of the preparations for the picnic and Pozzo's evident enjoyment of it. There is nothing jaded about Estragon's appetite. He is ravenous, and overcomes his normal timidity to satisfy his craving for the discarded chicken bone. There is an irony in Vladimir's scandalized remark to this. (p.27)

Immediate things like the need for food brook no delay and need instant remedy, even at the expense of good manners and decorum. Those who have waited so long for Godot must have basic desires met more swiftly.

In the second Act we have the same charade over the eating of the radish. The search for food implies action, and Estragon accepts the black and univiting radish rather than going to seek the carrot he would prefer.

Part of Vladimir's function in the play therefore seems to be as provider for his friend. He may not be able to provide food that is always to Estragon's liking, but at least he is able to nourish Estragon's body to some extent, as he does his mind in the endless points for debate he offers him.

Sleep and dreams

In the play sleep is denied Estragon almost as a form of torture. He is constantly settling down and being prodded into wakefulness by Vladimir. It is as though sleep, like death, implies a separation, and this neither of them can bear. Right at the start of the play Vladimir has asked, 'May one enquire where His Highness spent the night?', and there is a gap filled by sleep between the two acts. As well as being an escape from reality, sleep allows the tramps to dream. The dreams, however, must remain private, as Vladimir will have no share in them. He shouts at the top of his voice in a kind of terror, 'DON'T TELL ME.'

In the second Act Estragon finds the effort of trying to remember too much for him, and complains that he is tired. But he is forced into attention as Vladimir points out the leaves on the tree that have grown in the time he has slept. In the muddle of bodies on stage after the blind Pozzo has fallen and they all become hopelessly entangled, Estragon's solution is to have a snooze – and they do, indeed, fall asleep.

Later, when Pozzo and Lucky have made their final exit, Estragon once more takes comfort in sleep, but, as usual, this is short-lived. Vladimir wakes him, and Estragon asks him bitterly why he will never allow him to sleep. Once again the excuse for Vladimir's action is his loneliness, and again he refuses to listen to Estragon's dream. It is Vladimir, however, who is left to consider the whole theme of reality as opposed to the dream state: 'Was I sleeping, while the others suffered? Am I sleeping now?' Desperately he tries to establish the truth of his situation, yet he cannot bear the conclusion to which his thoughts are leading him.

Suffering

We have throughout the play the contrast between physical and spiritual suffering.

The sight of the running sore on Lucky's neck horrifies the tramps. This sign of his servitude causes them great concern, but with their usual attitude of acceptance they take it as inevitable. The contrast is thus so much the greater when they turn on Lucky and revile him for his treatment of Pozzo. Sympathy for Pozzo is in its turn short-lived, and his: '. . . and now . . . he's killing me' is lost in his speech of recovery:

(*calmer*) 'Gentlemen. I don't know what came over me . . . Forget all I said . . . Do I look like a man that can be made to suffer?'

It is the same character, remember, who is later begging for help in piteous tones as he grovels on the ground without the aid of his dumb menial. The tramps too have physical disabilities. Vladimir, with his weak bladder and hint of more serious disease, and Estragon with his painful feet, are constantly referring to their ailments.

Estragon especially has his share of receiving and giving pain. His attempt to be kind to Lucky is repaid by a kick on the shin. In Act 2, when the situation is different, Estragon has a chance of taking his revenge. In the event, however, it is he who suffers yet once more. (p.88).

There is no doubt, however, that in comparison even with the tramps, Lucky and Pozzo suffer the greater privations. Lucky is bereft of speech and Pozzo of sight, although the latter still retains his authority in spite of this. Suffering has to be endured. There is no escape for any of the characters in the play. On each occasion that it is suggested the tramps reject the idea of suicide. Neither sees any hope of success that way, and the notion is reduced to the level of farce with the falling of Estragon's trousers through lack of the rope that might have brought release from torment.

Biblical themes and references

From the opening gambit of Vladimir's account of the Crucifixion the play abounds in religious references and biblical imagery. The Bible is central to the meaning of the play.

On stage we have two creatures who, late in the action, are able to assert: 'We are men.' The audience is constantly being told that they are made in God's image, and these two scarecrows even have the effrontery to liken themselves to Christ:

Vladimir But you can't go barefoot!
Estragon Christ did.

Estragon hints at this idea too when he says in reply to Vladimir's taunt:

Estragon The best thing would be to kill me, like the other.
Vladimir What other? (*Pause*.) What other?'

But Estragon will not be drawn, and shrugs him off with a vague:

Like billions of others.

The cross itself is an image that is used in at least two tableaux in the play, and is a frequent point of reference. Vladimir berates Lucky for his treatment of Pozzo (a total reversal of the master/ servant situation):

Vladimir (*to Lucky*). 'How dare you! It's abominable! Such a good master! Crucify him like that!'

The idea of Christ on the Cross flanked by the two malefactors is taken up in Act 1 immediately after Lucky's long tirade. First we have the tableau of Lucky, supported by Estragon and Vladimir, then the stage direction *Vladimir and Estragon hoist Lucky to his feet, support him an instant, then let him go. He falls.*

We find the direct antithesis of this scene in Act 2, only this time it is Pozzo they are supporting:

Vladimir He wants us to help him get up.
Estragon Then why don't we? What are we waiting for?
They help Pozzo to his feet, let him go. He falls.
Vladimir We must hold him. (*They get him up again.*)

Then follows the significant stage direction *Pozzo sags between them, his arms round their necks.*
In each situation we have a reminder of the scene at Calvary, and in each case the tramps are set in supporting roles to the main protagonist.
The basic theme of waiting is itself supported by a text from the Book of Proverbs, 13, 12: 'Hope deferred maketh the heart sick, but when the desire cometh it is a tree of life', and as we have already remarked, the tree in the second part of the play has four or five leaves. To Vladimir at least this is a sign of hope.

There is no denying the fact of the tree's sprouting, even though there may be exaggeration in the extent of its foliage. One other biblical reference is worthy of note. The tramps return to the word-magic of proper names. This is the same game as that played by Ulysses in the cave of the Cyclops when he concealed his identity under the disguise of Noman, to the subsequent confusion of the giant. In Act 2, when Pozzo is down and at their mercy, they taunt him and cast further doubts on his identity:

Vladimir I tell you his name is Pozzo.

Estragon We'll soon see. (*He reflects.*) Abel! Abel!
Pozzo Help!
Estragon Got it in one!
Vladimir I begin to grow weary of this motif.
Estragon Perhaps the other is called Cain. Cain! Cain!

The terrible significance of the universality of the character should not be lost to us in Estragon's 'He's all humanity.'

Nor can we fail to hear in the whole play Cain's reply to God's question after the murder of his brother Abel: 'Where is thy brother Abel?' And he said, 'I know not: Am I my brother's keeper?' (Genesis, 4, 9.) Nor is Abel's punishment unlike that of the ever-wandering Pozzo and Lucky: 'A fugitive and a vagabond shalt thou be in the earth.' His acceptance of the situation is also like that of our two itinerants: 'I shall be a fugitive and a vagabond in the earth, and it shall come to pass, that every one that findeth me shall slay me.'

Structure and style

Structure

No matter how vague our notions may be, we all have some idea of what to expect from a dramatic performance. Many of us have been brought up on the pattern of plays showing the development of character; we have been stimulated by novel situations and kept interested by twists of plot. Poetry and music have effectively enlivened the duller moments of some plays for us – Shakespeare was a master of such devices. What then, with such a tradition behind us, are we to make of *Waiting for Godot*? It will help if we adopt the same approach that we need for the reading of modern poetry. Here too a long tradition teaches us what to expect. We look eagerly for rhyme, fixed metrical arrangement, rhythm, predictable stresses, but we frequently look in vain. In order to understand and appreciate this work a new conception of the nature and potential of poetry is essential. If we approach drama from a similar standpoint we can at least begin to understand *Waiting for Godot* more fully. What T. S. Eliot did for twentieth-century poetry in *The Waste Land*, Samuel Beckett did for the modern theatre in this play.

Waiting for Godot was first produced in Paris in 1953, and then in London in 1955. Mystified audiences tried to unravel the puzzle; the author himself forecast that it would play to empty houses. Indeed, Beckett's secret hope that such would be the case may be the key to understanding his motives in writing the play. In the event, however, *Waiting for Godot* was hugely successful. From its first performance it has attracted a spate of critics and interpreters; countless producers have added their ideas to presentation. We in turn have to consider how a play in which so little happens can hold audiences for three hours and send them home still discussing the experience. A recent television showing in America evoked the comment from one fireside critic: 'It was a play about two tramps in a desert and nothing happened.' This echoed a more serious and scholarly critic, Eva Metman, who suggested that the story concerned 'two tramps who dawdled in a barren place awaiting a rescuer from misery'. If we are looking for a story we are going to be disappointed; we must therefore be prepared to revise any preconceived notions we may have about what constitutes a play.

The boy in the Second Act, who claims to be on his first visit to the tramps, addresses Vladimir as Mr Albert, just as the first boy took similar liberties with identity. Within the pairs of characters we find the same balance. Vladimir is the incurable romantic, always harking back to the golden days. Estragon concerns himself with the moment, and cannot cope with immediate events. The relationship between the two tramps is one of intimacy, and they have been likened to a long-married couple who have grown so used to each other that they are too apathetic to bring their partnership to an end.

In Pozzo and Lucky we have the more formal situation of master and servant, with the traditional trappings of reward and punishment maintaining domination and subservience. The image of the rope which is used to bind Lucky is transferred in function to hold up Estragon's trousers, with frequent allusions to its more sinister possible use as a hangman's noose.

Beckett has been rightly praised for the symmetry of his work, and however inconsequential the dialogue of *Godot* may sound, the construction of the play has a definite pattern. There is a balance in each of the two Acts, and each Act complements the other. The tramps, Vladimir and Estragon, talk; Pozzo and Lucky enter and join the conversation; on their departure the boy appears with the news that Godot won't be coming that day.

Act 2 follows the pattern, the significant difference being that Pozzo is now blind and Lucky dumb. The only change in the scenery throughout is that in Act 2 we are told that the tree has sprouted four or five leaves.

Style

Vladimir and Estragon may look like tramps, but the topics they range over, and the smattering of foreign and classical languages they use, show them to be well above the level of most itinerant drop-outs.

Beckett makes use of a rapid interchange between them that carries us forward with its pace; short, sharp speeches of the nature of stichomythia which apparently do not advance the action but add detail to detail until the topic is exhausted. We find this first in Act One, when they are discussing the fate of the thieves at the crucifixion:

Estragon Who?
Vladimir What?
Estragon What's all this about? Abused who?
Vladimir The Saviour.
Estragon Why?
Vladimir Because he wouldn't save them.
Estragon From hell?
Vladimir Imbecile! From death.
Estragon I thought you said hell.
Vladimir From death, from death.

In this short exchange we have the idea of salvation and the equation of death and hell.

The Irishness of the tramps is brought out on occasion by the use of specifically Irish terms, although the two of them can be played as natives of Ireland throughout. Quite near the start of the play Estragon says, 'Stop blathering and help me off with this bloody thing.' (Act 1, p.10.) The word 'blather', or 'blether', is used frequently in Ireland and Scotland for the empty chattering that is likened to a bladder of wind. Indeed, the inflatable part of a football is still called a 'blether' in parts of Scotland.

Beckett, however, is not tempted to let the Irishness of the dialogue take over. He uses the nature of his countrymen, but is not prepared to submerge his message in their language. French, in which he was writing, imposed a discipline which left no room for the whimsical Irishry of a Synge or an O'Casey.

He is not averse, however, to poking fun at both the English and the French, and indeed at the kind of French the English invariably speak, as when Estragon says 'Calm ... calm ... The English say *cawm*.' – a line that is guaranteed to win a laugh from any audience. When the tramps are asked their opinion of Pozzo's speech about the night it is Vladimir who first catches the implication of his 'How did you find me?' with his answer 'Oh very good, very very good'. But from Estragon Pozzo wins the typically British Tommy's mock-French 'Oh tray bong, tray tray tray bong' with its extra 'very'. Every now and again we are reminded of the Irish speech rhythms and vocabulary. When the boy appears we hear him say, 'I mind the goats, sir.' with its idea of watching over the flocks and a link with biblical language.

Throughout the play there are Latin tags gleaned from the law and the philosophers. Qua – meaning 'as' or 'in the nature of' features prominently among these, and is found in Lucky's long speech, both for sound in a repetitive way as well as for legal overtones. When the blind Pozzo ponders his loss of sight Estragon urges him to say more of his deprivation.

'Expand! Expand!' he says. Vladimir bids him leave the man in peace because he is 'thinking of the days when he was happy: *Memoria praeteritorum bonorum* [A memory of the good things in times gone by].'

Comedy and stage-business

The tramps have been likened to Laurel and Hardy by some

critics, and to Charlie Chaplin by others. Perhaps there is something of the circus clown added for good measure. Much of the 'business' Beckett makes them enact is part of the stock-in-trade of the lighter side of the theatre. Boots will always be associated with Charlie Chaplin: there was even a song composed about his footwear; so, if the borrowing from the cinema is authentic, it is not strange to find Estragon fumbling with his boots right from the start of the play. The bowler-hat also was part of the wardrobe of these three film comedians, and it featured widely in many of their gags. Its distinctive shape, and the uses to which it could be put, make it an easy object of ridicule.

Beckett uses the protracted joke as part of his technique, and this too has been borrowed from comedians like Laurel and Hardy. Part of the charm (or irritation, depending on one's point of view) of their jokes was to be found in their repetitive nature and their predictability. A piano being delivered up a flight of steps finally made it to the top, before immediately hurtling down to its starting-point. We find a similar situation with the business of the hat being passed from one to the other in Act Two; there are twenty-four lines of stage-directions describing the sequence in the transfer of Lucky's hat from Vladimir to Estragon, and there is the inevitable climax of: *Estragon who takes it and hands it back to Vladimir who takes it and throws it down*. Perhaps even this piece of action is, for the audience, a welcome relief to the tedium – or maybe its repetitive nature plays on their nerve-endings until they are actually willing it to stop.

The arrival of Pozzo and Lucky gives additional scope for stage techniques borrowed from pantomime and burlesque. Lucky, as the one-end-of-the-ladder joke (though in this case it is a rope), is well across the stage before Pozzo appears. Just as their arrival is unexpected, so we are eager to know who is dominating this strangely cowed creature. The whip, symbol of authority, leaves us in no doubt about the relationship of the two. This domination is completed by the ballet of the picnic and the staccato parade-like orders barked out by the auto-cratic Pozzo to the robot-like Lucky. The overloaded servant has been part of the comedy scene since clowns first made their appearance. Here, however, it is the logical nature of the dropping and retrieving that adds to the effect. The precision is the same as that we find in the coke-stealing scene in Wesker's *Chips with Everything*. This is a skilfully planned piece of business, and no haphazard falling about. Later in the second Act we have the splendid knock-about comedy of Vladimir trying to look at Estragon's leg. (p.67)

Shortly after, there is a weird miming of the Pozzo and Lucky scene, with its strange, 'venereal' cursing: 'Gonococcus! Spirochaete!' (The bacterium causing gonorrhoea and the spiral organism of syphilis.) This is a prelude to the arrival of the strangely changed pair, the one blind and the other dumb, so that the two scenes are linked by a contrived mime. Part of the pantomime ploy used is the hiding-place that fails to conceal, with the joke being shared by the audience. Vladimir pushes Estragon towards the auditorium as a way of escape, but he recoils in horror.

The only other place of concealment is the tree, and that proves of little use – either for suicide or as a hiding-place.

Tableaux and silence

As we have seen, the stage setting for the play is as stark as the dialogue and as simple as the props. All our attention is focused on the actors. Every action is significant in a play where there is comparatively little movement.

From the opening of the curtain on the first Act we have sight of the tramps in characteristically indolent attitudes. Estragon is sitting on a low mound, making heavy weather of removing one of his boots. The effort proves abortive, and he rests. Vladimir approaches with a wide-legged walk and takes up his stance on stage. The only movement is that of the tramps looking inside boot or hat for foreign bodies. When they do eventually move it is with some effort, and they do so with difficulty, looking into wings or auditorium as though in search of something. Vladimir seems the more agitated of the two, and he can't bear the ease with which Estragon finds escape in sleep. His own weak bladder causes him to make frequent and rapid exits out of sight of the audience to the side of the stage. Estragon is at hand to encourage him and to mime his actions.

Throughout the early part of the scene there have appeared the words 'Pause' and 'Silence' in the stage-directions:

Vladimir '... This is getting alarming. (*Silence*). (*Vladimir deep in thought, Estragon pulling at his toes.*) One of the thieves was saved. (*Pause.*) It's a reasonable percentage. (*Pause.*) Gogo.'

It is as though a near-physical effort is needed to keep the dialogue going, and to elicit any kind of response from a partner.

Silence is used in a more positive fashion in the scene where the tramps think they hear Godot.

Vladimir Listen.
They listen, grotesquely rigid.
Estragon I hear nothing.
Vladimir Hssst! ... Nor I.

So we have the two statues stiff with anticipation and their silence shared by the audience, which is only able to relax when they do.

It is this kind of silence that is contrasted with the stage-direction *A terrible cry, close at hand*; when eventually, not Godot, but Pozzo and Lucky appear.

The eventual conversation between the tramps and Pozzo also has its share of silences. Pozzo, however, does not seem to be embarrassed by them. The other two 'say nothing', and the attempt at interchange dies in:

(*Silence*) It's of no importance. Let me see . . . (*He reflects*).

Pozzo himself is an adept at striking poses, particularly when he wants to attract and hold an audience. He uses his throat-spray to catch attention, as he has previously used the ritual of the filling and lighting of his pipe.

I am ready. Is everybody listening? Is everybody ready?

He is the dominating figure in the tableau as they look at the sky.

Pozzo A great calm descends. (*Raising his hand.*) Listen! Pan sleeps.

In violent contrast to such scenes we have the unleashed fury of Lucky's tirade and the frantic efforts of the rest to stifle him and restore peace once more.

The Act ends in the tableau of the tramps in silence, having decided to go but not moving.

The second Act continues the theme of silence.

In the dialogue between Vladimir and Estragon that follows there are significant stage-directions: *Silence*, and *Long Silence*. It is as though Beckett is making a stylized punctuation of the silences. This would seem to be in accord with the production at the Royal Court Theatre, supervised by the author and using his English text. Here the farcical element was played down, and the pathos of the last few moments in each act emphasized the more.

At the end of the play we have Estragon asleep and Vladimir interrogating the boy about the nature of Godot. After the lad runs off we have:

Silence . . . Vladimir stands motionless and bowed.

It is this picture that we take with us as we leave the theatre.

Characters

The Enigma of Godot

Beckett's play has gained universal recognition as the one in which the title character never appears. It is not surprising, therefore, that many attempts have been made to identify Godot and to elucidate the mystery of the play.

The author himself when asked who Godot was said enigmatically, 'If I knew I would have said so in the play', the implication behind the statement being that he has done just that, and made clear who or what Godot was.

Godot's non-arrival provides the only fact we have in the whole play, although we learn certain things about him.

The tramps see him as being able to give them comfort. They look forward to being taken to his farm and being allowed 'to sleep, warm and dry with a full stomach – on straw'. The impression is that he is paternalistic, almost patriarchal, like the God of the Old Testament, meting out punishment and reward. His beard (which, according to the messenger may be white), adds to this impression of him. We may even picture him as portrayed by William Blake in one of his etchings. He does seem to have the human failing of favouritism, as he beats one of the messengers but not the other. Through their occupations he seems to divide the sheep from the goats, a strong echo from the Old Testament.

He is obviously a figure to be feared, as the tramps constantly cower at his impending approach, and there is no doubt that there is an element of the judge in him.

However much we may play with linguistics and phonetics and point out that the play was first written in French, and the emphasis of pronunciation therefore would have fallen on the second syllable of the name, we still have sympathy with the critic who forthrightly solved the problem: 'Godot – is God'. Over-simplified as such a solution may be, we cannot deny that there is much of the Deity in him.

Perhaps it is as well for us to take what meaning we want from the character, and to have our own ideas about the person of Godot. The author has every right to point to the work itself as his solution of the puzzle.

Vladimir

When I think of it ... all these years ... but for me ... where would you be ...?

Vladimir is the dominating personality. He takes his responsibility for Estragon seriously: 'It's too much for one man' (p.10), and he voices the text of the sermon of the play: One of the thieves was saved. It is through him that we follow the idea of salvation as a theme. He is the religious one, the seeker after truth; while Estragon contents himself with the pictures and colourful maps of his Bible (p.12), Vladimir ponders its philosophy and religious message. Estragon, almost wilfully stupid, serves as a foil, a foolish child for whom everything must be reduced to its simplest terms. He dismisses the idea of salvation and the universal obtuseness with which the idea is received: 'People are bloody ignorant apes' (p.13), although he seems to be one of them. When the tramps contemplate splitting up Vladimir has scant hope for Estragon's survival or determination to strike out on his own. It is to Vladimir that Estragon cries plaintively like a child when he is disturbed suddenly from sleep; it is to him also, as the provider, that Estragon looks for food. As the father-figure he is expected to provide the answer to any perplexing question:

Vladimir How do you mean tied?
Estragon Down.
Vladimir But to whom. By whom?

Estragon To your man.
Vladimir To Godot? Tied to Godot? What an idea!

No question of it. (*Pause*) For the moment. (pp.20–1) There
is special significance in the fact that Estragon calls Godot
'your man', as though the sole responsibility for their waiting
rests on Vladimir. Nor must we miss the importance of
Vladimir's 'For the moment.'

When Pozzo and Lucky first appear it is Vladimir who
proves himself the man of action. Estragon plucks him back
from going to Lucky's aid when he falls; later he is the first
to show compassion for Lucky's treatment and condition
(p.27). Later still he finds the presence of Pozzo distasteful,
and it is now his turn to make the suggestion, 'Let's go', and
Estragon who holds him back with 'We're in no hurry' (p.28).

When we reach the point of Lucky's entertainment it is
Vladimir who prefers the intellectual diversion: 'I'd like well
to hear him think' (p.39). Vladimir, by putting the hat back
on Lucky's head, seems to set free the spate of words which
issues forth in his long, quasi-philosophical oration. Indeed, it
is only when the headgear is removed that Lucky relapses
into his accustomed silence. Vladimir takes the initiative in
the conversation with the Boy, though Estragon foresees nothing but complications. There is no doubt, however, that it is
Mr Albert, the name to which Vladimir responds, who is
being sought out by Godot's messenger. He also retains a note
of optimism near the end of Act One when he tells Estragon:
'Tomorrow everything will be better' (p.52). When that tomorrow comes it is he who recalls the events of the previous
day and recapitulates for Estragon and the audience the
actions of Pozzo and Lucky.

In the second Act Vladimir once more serves as comforter
to the frightened Estragon as he awakens from a nightmare-
ridden sleep. Previously he has fed him, this time with a
more exotic root, a radish, which has not been to his liking.

Again in this Act it is Vladimir who first shows compassion, though this time it is for Pozzo, who is now blind, but Estragon still thinks that Godot himself has arrived.

Faced by a new situation when they can be of some help, Vladimir grasps the opportunity: 'Let us do something, while we have the chance! It is not every day that we are needed' (p.79). It is predictable that their efforts to help will be frustrated in a tangle of fallen bodies.

Just before the final arrival of the Boy, Vladimir makes a despairing attempt to rationalize their situation, and introduces the startling image of birth astride an open grave, thereby telescoping the whole of man's life into a very brief span indeed. This time it is he who recognizes the moment of challenge with 'Off we go again', as he greets Godot's messenger boy. He too is given the last word about salvation, his personal theme (p.94).

Estragon

'Beat me, certainly they beat me.'

From the start he seems doomed to suffer. It would appear that Estragon somehow provokes hostility by his unthinking actions, and Vladimir feels that he could avert retaliation by dealing with first causes. Throughout the play Estragon seeks escape in sleep, but is always ushered back to stark reality and seeks comfort from Vladimir. Yet often it is the latter who denies him the rest he needs.

It is his childish logic that prevents their first attempt at suicide by hanging from the bough of the barren tree. He realizes that he, being the lighter, will probably succeed, and that consequently Vladimir, the heavier, will break the bough, survive and be left lonely. In the encounter with Pozzo he is quick to deny any acquaintance with Godot. Although he is such a timid creature, he is not averse to asking Pozzo for the chicken bones, and much of his time is taken up with requests for food. Like Kipling's Kim, he is prepared to let anyone acquire merit by helping him to charity, whether it be Vladimir or Pozzo. Similar helpful action on his part does not seem to be so successful, and a bruised shin seems to be his only reward for going to wipe Lucky's tears. Not surprisingly there is an Irish exaggeration about 'I'll never walk again!' as he nurses his leg (p.32).

Estragon shows his first aggressive tendency in his conversation with the Boy – here he is at his most forcible: 'Approach when you're told, can't you?' When he shakes the Boy's arm Vladimir orders him to let the latter alone; Estragon's only excuse is, 'I'm unhappy'.

It is Estragon who makes an unprovoked attack on Lucky – though Vladimir fully concurs (pp.78–9) – when he is lying inert and unable to defend himself. It is only the pain this gives him in his own foot that makes Estragon stop. He resorts to his cure for all ills – sleep – and on being wakened once more by Vladimir protests yet again, 'Why will you never let me sleep?'

Just before the end of the play it is Estragon who, perhaps unwittingly, suggests the answer to their dilemma. Godot has again failed to materialize, and he says:

'And if we dropped him?' (*Pause*) 'If we dropped him?'

But it is no use, there is no answer here after all:

Vladimir 'He'd punish us.'

It is to Estragon that the last chance of action is given in the play: 'Yes, let's go.' The stage direction, *They do not move* clearly shows that they are bound to the wheel of time and the cycle is about to commence once more.

Pozzo and Lucky

These two are inextricably bound together. They act and react on each other in a special way. We see Lucky first, laden with luggage and tethered by a rope. His condition certainly belies his name, for he is driven by Pozzo, who is still in the wings when the rope is at full stretch. Apart from the luggage, the whip is the main prop at this point in the play.

Pozzo expects to be recognized by the two tramps, and quickly catches up the name of Godot, for whom Estragon at least has mistaken him. It transpires that he owns the land on which they are waiting. There is a great deal of stage business while Pozzo settles himself to his picnic; this gives the tramps an opportunity to inspect Lucky, who gives the impression of an overworked horse. The rope has caused a running sore on his neck, but he is 'not bad looking', as Vladimir points out (p.25). They are unsuccessful in getting any response from him other than the prolonged stare he gives Estragon at the request for the chicken bone. Pozzo makes great play of the tramps' waiting for Godot; he toys with the name as his own name has already been played with, and stuns Vladimir with his suggestion that Godot has their future in his hands. How has he come to such a conclusion on so little evidence? Is he in Godot's confidence?

There is a subtle change of relationship between the protagonists at this point, which does not go unnoticed by Pozzo. The tramps, deferential and fearful as we saw them at the first encounter, are now emboldened to ask a question as equals, and it is remarked that no good will come of this. Pozzo prepares to answer the question put to him about Lucky in the manner of the most temperamental prima donna, and shows all the attributes of the professional politician. He strikes a pose, and waits to become the full focus of attention.

Like many another public speaker, he loses his train of thought and has to be prompted by Vladimir and Estragon, who mime the plight of Lucky. We reach the nub of the relationship between these two when Pozzo says, 'Remark that I might just as well have been in his shoes and he in mine' (p.31). We are soon made aware, however, of Pozzo's dependence on his servants, and the debt he owes him: 'But for him all my thoughts, all my feelings, would have been of common things' (p.33).

In an emotional outburst we learn of Pozzo's suffering at the hands of Lucky and his need to be rid of him, but he is able to regain control, and we are left wondering whether indeed, considering their rôles, the master can be made to suffer at the hands of the servant.

As a reward for their civility and patience the tramps are to be beguiled by a dance and an oration from Lucky. The one is as short as the other is long and breathless. This is Lucky's great virtuoso moment, and he turns himself on and off like a tap. Theatrically the effect is as startling as the shock of white hair which appears when he takes off his hat, or the contrasting baldness of Pozzo when he removes his headgear. The scene ends with the exaggerated civilities of leave-taking and the continued dominance of Pozzo over his slave.

In the second Act the roles of the two are as before, but Pozzo in his blindness is more deeply dependent on Lucky. The bully has lost much of his arrogance, and now looks for pity. The tramps consider the possibility of going to Pozzo's aid, unaware, apparently, that he is blind. They accept this fact without comment when they are told, as they accept everything that happens to them without question.

It is Vladimir's probing of Pozzo that finally brings the former's great outburst about time and the transience of the human condition. The dumb Lucky and the blind Pozzo leave the stage, and all we have as a memory of them is the sound of yet another fall that leaves them waiting off-stage for whoever may be willing to go to their aid.

A Boy

There may be one Boy, two Boys, or an infinite series of them stretching back or extending forward until Godot arrives. Towards the end of Act 1 a Boy makes his timid entrance on to the stage. He has evidently been expected, since Estragon asks him what has kept him so late. He appears to have been waiting uncertainly for some time, and the suggestion is that he has been frightened of Pozzo and Lucky, the whip and the noise.

Vladimir eventually tries to pin down the Boy's identity as the same one who had been there the previous day. He denies this, and says that this is his first visit. The lad delivers his message in a burst of words, and promises faithfully that Godot will be coming the next day. Vladimir cross-questions him about his relationship with Godot and about his own occupation. He appears to be the goat-herd, while his brother looks after the sheep. He is Godot's favourite, as it is his brother who seems to get the beatings. He has genuine doubts to his own happiness, but accepts his state of life. The message he has to take back to Godot concerns the actual existence of the two tramps. He has seen them, hasn't he? Then that is the message he must carry to Godot.

In Act 2 a Boy enters evidently seeking Vladimir, whom he addresses as 'Mr Albert' (as also in Act 1 – p.49). Although he recognizes the tramp, he seems not to be the same Boy as the messenger of the previous day. Vladimir questions him about Godot, and it transpires that Godot does not actually *do* anything; and that he has a beard, possibly white. Vladimir expresses deep concern at the second piece of information with the heartfelt 'Christ have mercy on us!' (p.92). Once again the message to be carried back to Godot concerns the existence of the two tramps and the reality of the meeting with the Boy. The lad finally eludes the lunge Vladimir makes at him, and runs off into the night.

The Nameless Ones

These characters, like Godot, never appear on stage, but we have the feeling that they are not far away throughout the action.

At the start of Act 1 we hear that they have beaten Estragon, and that they have done this before. They are called 'The same lot as usual.'

In Act 2, after Estragon has again been parted from Vladimir, we hear that he has once more been beaten. He now numbers his assailants, and says that there were ten of them. Truth being at something of a premium in this play, we are at liberty either to accept or reject this number of attackers. Perhaps, like Falstaff at the Gadshill ambush, a monstrous regiment has grown out of a few men. But at any rate, a specific number is mentioned, and an exact incident suggested. Such accuracy is rare in the play, and is thus worthy of note. We hear of these assailants once again, when Vladimir is urging Estragon to attack Lucky. He reminds him that it was Lucky who had kicked him the previous day, to which Estragon replies, 'I tell you there was ten of them' (p.79). But even with the odds at two to one, Vladimir needs the victim to be asleep before he can consider the possibility of success.

Textual notes and revision questions

As long ago as 1953 Raymond Williams commented on the simplicity of the everyday speech used in *Waiting for Godot*. As we are dealing with relatively basic people the speech, for the most part, follows that pattern and is reasonably straightforward. Every so often, however, we have some of the verbal juggling that we find in the words of James Joyce, and some ideas lurk behind the surface meaning of the words used. The following list follows the sequence of the play and may be of some assistance.

Act 1

blathering To talk nonsense, to babble.

I'd like to hear what you'd say if you had what I have He has a condition caused, probably, by enlargement of the prostate gland.

AP-PALLED The division of the word is deliberate, with its connotation with pall and hearse.

privation The condition of being without something formerly or properly possessed.

insinuating Suggesting, implying.

bawd Woman in charge of the girls in a brothel, or house of ill fame.

pugilist Fist-fighter.

Where it fails mandrakes grow It was a belief that when a man was hanged he ejaculated, and where the sperm fell a mandrake would grow. The mandrake through its forked shape was likened to the human, and particularly the male, form. It was thought to have magical properties, and shrieked like a human when pulled from the ground.

supplication Prayer, plea.

vacuously Without any expression.

magnanimous Open-hearted, generous.

voraciously Greedily.

chafing Rubbing.

slaver Saliva issuing from the mouth.

goitre Enlargement of the thyroid gland in the throat, shown as swelling.

knook (Fr. *un knouk*) A word invented by Beckett. According to Professor Colin Duckworth, it was formed on the analogy of the Russian word knout, a whip or knotted rope.

dudeen Irish for short clay tobacco pipe.

farandole A lively dance of Provençal origin.

fandango A Spanish-American dance in triple time.

aesthete Someone highly sensitive towards the Arts.

pulverizer A machine to reduce stone etc. to dust and powder.

apathia Stoicism, freedom from emotion.

athambia Astonishment, fearlessness.

aphasia Lack of the faculty of speech, as a result of brain damage.

the divine Miranda Prospero's daughter in *The Tempest*.

Acacacacademy of Anthropopopometry Anthropometry is a science based on human measurement.

in Possy *In posse*, potential, possible.

in Essy *In esse*, being, alive.

alimentation Nourishment.

defecation Disposal of waste body-matter; excretion.

camogie Irish hurling.

per caput Per head.

Bishop Berkeley 1685–1755. He postulated that if God does not exist, the existence of the universe itself and of mankind is very doubtful.

half-hunter Generally gold watch. Demi-hunter: a watch having a hunting case, with a hole in the lid permitting the time to be told when the lid is closed.

Revision questions on Act 1

1 What is the significance of the mention of the Eiffel Tower at this point in the play, and later in the Act?

2 What difference do you find in the tramps' approach to the Bible in this scene? What significance do you see in this?

3 Why do you think Vladimir is so adamant about not being told Estragon's dream?

4 List the qualities of Lucky that reduce him to the level of an animal.

5 Describe the appearance of Lucky from comments made by the others about him.

6 Follow closely the change in attitude of Vladimir and Estragon towards Pozzo.

7 What reason does Pozzo put forward for Lucky's not putting down his luggage?

8 What is the significance of Pozzo's description of the sky at this point in the play? Look closely at his speech, and attempt a critical appraisal.

9 What do you think Lucky is trying to say in his long speech? Make some attempt to comment on its dramatic significance.

10 What is the dramatic purpose of the entrance of the messenger Boy at the end of the Act?

Act 2

Macon country Mâcon is in E. Central France.
puked Been sick; vomited.
charnel-house Repository for dead bodies.
foetal Like a child in the womb.
coquettishly Like a girl flirting light-heartedly.
Punctilious Strict on the observance of detail.
Morpion Estragon seems to have concocted this word to keep the rhythm flowing.
Cretin One suffering from a lack of thyroid; an idiot.

congeners Person or thing nearly related or similar to another.

Look at the little cloud There seems to be no point in this statement until we remember 1 Kings, 18, 43–4, with Elijah on Mount Carmel: 'And [Elijah] said to his servant, Go up now, look toward the sea. And he went up, and looked, and said, There is nothing. And he said, Go again seven times. And it came to pass at the seventh time, that he said, Behold there ariseth a little cloud out of the sea, like a man's hand . . .'

Perhaps he can see into the future Tiresias or another blind prophet saw Pallas Athene bathing, and was splashed with water and blinded. Later the goddess repented and gave him the power of soothsaying.

caryatids A caryatid is a female figure used in a column and for support.

Revision questions on Act 2

1 What is the importance of Estragon's boots at this point in the play?

2 What has happened to Estragon between the Acts? Discuss the importance of your answer.

3 Follow the steps in Vladimir's attempt to remind Estragon of what happened the previous day.

4 Trace the development of thought that leads Estragon to say, 'That wasn't such a bad little canter.'

5 What is the importance of Lucky's hat in this Act?

6 Enumerate the mimes performed by Vladimir and Estragon in this Act.

7 Explain what Vladimir means by, 'In anticipation of some tangible return.' How do the tramps go about getting this?

8 What does Estragon mean when he says of Pozzo, 'He's all humanity'?

9 What significance is there in the tramps' treatment of Lucky?

10 What is the dramatic importance of the entry of the messenger boy in this Act?

General questions

1 What difficulties would you consider might face a producer of *Waiting for Godot*?

2 Contrast the roles of Vladimir and Estragon in the play.

3 Write an essay on the structure of *Waiting for Godot*.

4 'Let us do something while we have the chance.' Develop this idea as you find it in the play.

5 'He's all humanity.' How closely does this in fact relate to Pozzo?

6 What is Lucky's role in the play?

7 What is the function of the boy in each of the acts?

8 'A play in which nothing happens – twice.' Show by a close study of the play that quite a lot happens on stage.

9 What do you find to be the significance of Lucky's dumbness and Pozzo's blindness?

10 'Although he never appears, Godot serves a vital purpose in the play.' What is that purpose?

11 Analyse closely the long speech of Lucky, and try to paraphrase it.

12 Would you prefer to read this play or to see it acted? Support your preference.

13 What do you think was behind Beckett's hope that *Waiting for Godot* would play to empty houses? Try to account for the success of the play.

14 Write an essay on the stage devices used in the play. e.g. the business of the hats, Lucky and his luggage etc. Do you find them effective?

15 Write a comparison of the two Acts of the play.

16 Try to account for the bewilderment felt by some of the early audiences when confronted with this play.

17 Consider the term tragi-comedy in relation to the play.

18 'Beckett's plays abound in religious imagery and thought.' Consider this aspect of the play.

19 'Godot remains off stage, a mysterious and dwindling source of hope.' Do you find any hope in the play?

20 'Nothing to be done' is the message of *Waiting for Godot*. Do you agree?